CRITTERS OF ARIZONA POCKET GUIDE

oduced in cooperation with Wildlife Forever

by Ann E. McCarthy, Director of Education

Adventure Publications, Inc.
Cambridge, Minnesota

Dedication

To Ryan, Madison, Alexandra, Chase and Alexis and tomorrow's land stewards, and to BOP-BOP and the Zb▮ Family who truly treasure the natural beauty unique to Ari▮

— Ann E. McC▮

Research and Editorial Assistance: David A. Frederick

Technical Editor: Arizona Game and Fish Department

Cover, interior design and illustrations: Jonathan Norberg

Photo Credits: **George Andrejko/AZ Fish and Game Dept.:** 20, 2▮ (male) **Mike Barlow/DPA:** 24 (male), 44 **Erwin and Peggy Bau▮ BillMarchel.com:** 60 (both) **Rick and Nora Bowers:** 100 **Dominique** ▮ 72 (perching) **Dominique Braud/DPA:** 36 (female & cubs), 66 **Collins:** 88 (female) **Sharon Cummings/DPA:** 18, 102 **Rob Cur▮ Image Finders:** 96 (male) **E. R. Degginger/DPA:** 42, 74 **Dudley Edmo▮** 28, 72 (soaring), 80 (both), 86 (both), 104 (soaring) **Darrell Guli▮** 34 **Ned Harris:** 64 (both) **Richard Haug:** 38 **Adam Jones:** 108 **K▮ Karlson:** 62 **Larry Kimball/Pronghorn Photo:** 106 (female) **Gr▮ Lasley/KAC Productions:** 30, 32 **Bill Lea/DPA:** 14, 46 **B▮ Magnuson/Pronghorn Photo:** 106 (male) **Steve and Dave Maslows▮ Anthony Mercieca:** 84 (both) **John Mielcarek/DPI:** 22 **Skip Mood▮** 12, 36 (male) **Alan Nelson/DPA:** 10, 16, 52 **Stan Osolinski/DP▮** (female), 50 (female), 54 **John Pennoyer:** 88 (male) **Rod Planck/DP▮** 98 **Fritz Polking/DPA:** 82 **Jim Roetzel/DPA:** 48 **Stan Tekiela:** 68, 7▮ 92, 94 **Connie Toops:** 96 (female) **John & Gloria Tveten/KAC Produ▮** 58 **Brian K. Wheeler:** 76 (both), 104 (perching)

DPA: Dembinsky Photo Associates

Second Printing
Copyright 2002 by Wildlife Forever
Published by Adventure Publications, Inc.
820 Cleveland Street South
Cambridge, MN 55008, 1-800-678-7006
All rights reserved
Printed in China
ISBN 1-59193-001-4

ABOUT WILDLIFE FOREVER

...ife Forever is a nonprofit conservation organization ded-
...d to conserving America's wildlife heritage through
...ation, preservation of habitat and management of fish
...wildlife. Working at the grassroots level, Wildlife Forever
...completed conservation projects in all 50 states. Wildlife
...ver's innovative outreach programs include the Wildlife
...ver State-Fish Art Project and the Theodore Roosevelt
...ervation Alliance.

...of the Wild

...e "cry of the wild" can still be heard across this great land.
...ave heard the bugle of an elk amid the foothills of the west-
...n plains...the shrill of a bald eagle along the banks of the
...ighty Mississippi...the roar of a brown bear on windswept
...ndra...the thunder of migrating waterfowl on coastal
...ores...the gobble of a wild turkey among eastern hard-
...ods and the haunting cry of a sandhill crane in the
...etlands of the Central Flyway. America is truly blessed–a
...nd rich in natural resources. This legacy must be pre-
...rved.

...ope this book will provide you with an insight to the many
...onders of the natural world and serve as a stepping-stone
...the great outdoors.

...urs for wildlife...forever,

...uglas H. Grann
...esident & CEO,
...ldlife Forever

To learn more contact us at
763-253-0222, 2700
Freeway Blvd., Ste. 1000,
Brooklyn Center, MN 55430
or check out our website at
www.wildlifeforever.org.

TABLE OF CONTENTS

About Wildlife Forever . . . .
Foreword by Director Shroufe. . . . .
Facts About Arizona. . . . .
How to Use This Guide . . . .

Mammals

Badger . . . .
Bat, Occult Little Brown . . . .
Bear, Black . . . .
Beaver . . . .
Bobcat . . . .
Cottontail, Desert . . . .
Coyote. . . . .
Deer, Mule . . . .
Deer, White-tailed . . . .
Elk . . . .
Fox, Gray . . . .
Jackrabbit, Black-tailed . . . .
Javelina. . . . .
Lion, Mountain . . . .
Muskrat . . . .
Otter, River . . . .
Porcupine. . . . .
Pronghorn. . . . .
Raccoon . . . .
Ringtail . . . .
Sheep, Desert Bighorn. . . . .
Skunk, Striped. . . . .
Squirrel, Round-tailed Ground . . . .
Wolf, Mexican Gray . . . .
Woodrat, White-throated. . . . .

s

ackbird, Red-winged. 61
uebird, Mountain 63
ndor, California 65
ot, American 67
ane, Sandhill 69
ve, Mourning. 71
gle, Bald 73
con, Peregrine 75
wk, Cooper's 77
wk, Red-tailed. 79
wk, Sharp-shinned 81
ron, Great Blue 83
mmingbird, Anna's 85
strel, American 87
allard 89
eadowlark, Western. 91
l, Great Horned. 93
l, Western Burrowing. 95
ail, Gambel's 97
bin, American 99
whee, Abert's 101
rkey, Wild. 103
lture, Turkey 105
odpecker, Gila. 107
en, Cactus. 109
st 110
Words. 116
ife Forever Projects in Arizona 124
r. 125

FOREWORD

by Duane Shroufe,
Director, Arizona Game and Fish Department

Isn't Arizona grand! From the Grand Canyon on the Utah [bor]der to the vast sand dunes in Yuma, from the snow-cov[ered] peaks in Flagstaff to the grassland along the Mexican bo[rder], Arizona has it all! As Director, I want to encourage ever[yone] to "Step Outside" and enjoy Arizona's great outdoors.

The incredible variety of habitats, ranging from tund[ra to] desert, supports an amazing assortment of wildlife. Pa[rt of] the mission of the Arizona Game and Fish Department [is to] conserve, enhance and restore Arizona's wildlife and h[abi]tats through protection and management. One are[a in] which history is being made is that of the California Co[ndor] Recovery Program. There are now more condors in the [wild] in Arizona than existed in the entire world in 1982. We [are] also bringing back the Mexican gray wolf and many o[ther] species of wildlife that have had trouble maintaining p[opu]lations in Arizona.

So, for present and future generations of wildlife and [peo]ple, I wish to thank each of you for supporting the Ari[zona] Game and Fish Department in its efforts. Together, we [are] making a difference. This book is dedicated to the e[njoy]ment of Arizona wildlife and the resources we all love.

Duane Shroufe
Director, Arizona Game and Fish Department

FACTS
About Arizona

na. The name means "little spring" and comes from either
'ima Indian people or the Papago Indian people. The nat-
beauty and landscape of painted deserts, gaping canyons,
-covered peaks, green valleys and dense forests have
ed the character, tradition and culture of Arizona.

na is the only place in North America where four deserts
e together. These deserts are the Mohave, Great Basin,
uahuan and Sonoran, which contains a greater diversity of
fe than any other desert in the U.S. While desert covers 2/3
e land, Arizona is also home to expansive Ponderosa Pine
Douglas Fir forests.

ured national parks, monuments and forests including
d Canyon National Park, Saguaro Nation Monument and
nado National Forest contain amazing beauty in their red-
formations, foothills, buttes, wildflowers, endless blue
, towering pines and dense stands of cottonwood, willow
box elder.

na's arid landscape provides healthy habitat for countless
ies of wildlife including bighorn sheep, Mexican gray wolf,
ghorn, elk, mule deer, black bear, javelina, Gambel's Quail,
Turkey, Sandhill Crane, Burrowing Owl, Bald Eagle and oth-
The rich habitat diversity in southeastern Arizona supports
species of hummingbirds than anywhere else in the U.S.

rs, skiers, hunters, anglers and rafters all enjoy miles of
and acres of wilderness. People who love the great out-
s love Arizona.

Amphibian: Arizona Tree Frog **State Bird:** Cactus Wren
Butterfly: Two-tailed Swallowtail **State Fish:** Arizona/Apache Trout
Flower: Saguaro Cactus Bloom **State Gemstone:** Turquoise
Mammal: Ringtail **State Nickname:** Grand Canyon State
Reptile: Arizona Ridge-nosed Rattlesnake **State Tree:** Palo Verde

HOW TO USE THIS GUIDE

While this book is not intended as a field guide (we d
want anyone getting too close to a bear trying to identi
species!), it is intended to be a great reference for info
tion on some of the fascinating animals that we loosely
the "critters" of Arizona. We think that the more informa
people have about wildlife and their needs, the more we
do to conserve this wonderful part of our natural world

Notes About Icons

In the mammal section, the track of
foot is included near the bottom rig
the page. The size, from top to bot
is included. When appropriate, the
and hind print are included with
front placed at the top of the oval,
the hind at the bottom. Note that for some animals, you
find that the hind print actually appears ahead of the f
This will be apparent in the layout of the tracks as show
the right margin. While the sizes of the individual tracks
relative to each other, the pattern of tracks is not. We w
have needed a very large page to accommodate the co
tracks compared to the round-tailed ground squ

The animal/person silhouette on the
tom left of the mammal pages is to s
the relative size of the animal comp
to an average-sized adult. Somet
it's easier to judge comparisons
actual measurements.

nocturnal (active at night)

diurnal (active during the day)

crepuscular (most active at dawn and dusk)

Z_zz *hibernates* (hibernates during the winter)

yellow symbols depicting the sun, moon or the sun on
horizon indicate whether the animal is nocturnal, diurnal
crepuscular. While you may see these animals at other
s, they are most active during the periods shown. The
w Zzzs indicate whether or not the animal hibernates.
e critters are true hibernators, which means they slow
body processes down a great deal and require very little
gy to survive the winter. Other critters are partial hiber-
rs, and they slow their body processes down only a little
require greater amounts of energy to survive the winter.

cup   ground   platform   cavity

he bird pages, the nest type is shown at the bottom
. This indicates whether the bird builds a cup-type nest,
und nest, a platform nest or a cavity nest.

he Lifelist on page 110, place a check by each mammal
'd you've seen, whether in your backyard or at the zoo.

DID YOU KNOW...? The badger uses its digging ability to d itself out of trouble. It can dig at a faster rate than a person ca dig with a shovel. While digging, the badger sends dirt flyi 4-5' into the air. Although the badger has very short legs a walks in a pigeon-toed fashion (toes pointed in), it can s reach speeds of 10-15 mph.

nocturnal

BADGER
Taxidea taxus

Size: body 20-35" long; tail 4-6" long; stands 9" high at shoulder; weighs 13-30 lbs.

abitat: grasslands, woodland edges and brushy fields

Range: throughout Arizona

Food: snakes, chipmunks, ground squirrels, rabbits, turtle eggs and ground-nesting birds' eggs; may burrow into dens of some of these prey

Mating: August to September; gestation of about 7 months (after a delayed period after mating)

Den: grass-lined; located 2-6' underground

Young: 3-7 young born blind; eyes open at 4-6 weeks; nurse for 4-6 weeks; later learn to hunt; independent at 10-12 weeks

dators: mountain lion, occasionally bear

Tracks: show 5 toes and a soft, medium-sized pad, with long claw imprints

scription: The badger has a wide, flattened body with t fur that is silver-gray to yellowish gray. It has a broad, ge-shaped head with a white stripe that runs from the , over the head and down the back. It has short rful legs with 2" claws and spends most of the underground.

mammals

2¼"

DID YOU KNOW...? The bat is the only mammal capable of flight. It uses echolocation (sound waves) to detect and catch insects. It is capable of catching 600 moths in one hour and thousands of mosquitoes in a single night. Each fall, as temperatures begin to drop and the numbers of insects decline, they migrate to favorite hibernation sites and return to breeding sites in late spring.

nocturnal   crepuscular   Zzz hibernator

BAT, OCCULT LITTLE BROWN
Myotis lucifugus occultus

Size: 3-4½" in length with a 1½" forearm; 8-9" wingspan; weighs ¼-⅓ of an ounce

Habitat: wooded areas primarily near water and large insect populations

Range: Mogollan Rim into Sky Islands of southeast Arizona

Food: insects including moths, mosquitoes and beetles

Mating: prior to hibernation each fall; gestation of 60 days (after a delayed period of 7 months after mating)

Roost Site: colonize and roost in groups in attics and other buildings, exfoliating (peeling) bark, tree cavities and caves

Young: one pup is born, commonly in maternity colonies of 300-600 females; weighs 30% of adult and nurses for approximately 4-6 weeks; able to fly at 3 weeks

Predators: owl, snake, raccoon, ringtail and domestic cat

Tracks: none

Description: The occult little brown bat has a coat of silky cinnamon-buff to dark brown hair, with pale gray undersides and hand-like wings. It skims the water's surface where it catches insects at a rate of one every eight seconds.

no tracks

mammals

DID YOU KNOW...? The black bear is an excellent climber can run at speeds of 25 mph. It loves honey and will rip op a beehive to obtain it. Its thick coat protects it from bee stin During winter, the black bear spends up to three months in den, living off its stored body fat.

 crepuscular **Zzz** *partial hibernator*

BEAR, BLACK
Ursus americanus

Size: body 4½-5' long; stands 2-3' high at shoulder; weighs 250-300 lbs.

Habitat: chapparal, pinyon-juniper and coniferous forests in mountainous areas

Range: northeast, central and southeast Arizona

Food: nuts, roots, berries, insects, mice and other small mammals, fish and garbage

Mating: June to July; gestation of about 60 days (after a delayed period of 5 months after mating)

Den: brush piles, hollow logs, under fallen trees, beneath uprooted trees or on rocky hillsides

Young: cubs emerge in April; cubs, usually twins, born blind and hairless with pinkish skin; 8" long; 8 oz. each; eyes open at 40 days; cubs nurse and remain in den until spring; independent at 18 months

Predators: adult male black bear may prey on cubs

Tracks: note big toe on outside of foot

Description: Fur is usually black, but it can be light brown, blonde or reddish brown. It marks trees with scent and fur. Torn apart logs and destroyed hornet nests may be signs of where bears have been.

4"

7-9"

DID YOU KNOW...? A beaver can chew down hundreds trees each year. One family of beavers may consume as mu as a ton (2,000 lbs.) of inner (cambium) bark in a single w ter. To maintain water levels, beavers may build dams up to 1 yards long. The beaver is specially adapted to life underwa with waterproof fur, webbed feet, goggle-like eyelids, and no and ear flaps. It's able to hold its breath for 15 minutes.

nocturnal   *crepuscular*

BEAVER
Castor canadensis

Size: body 27-35" long; tail 15" long, 7" wide; weighs 28-75 lbs.

Habitat: fresh water streams, rivers, ponds or lakes bordered by trees, usually willow and cottonwood

Range: throughout Arizona's waterways

Food: in spring and summer, leaves, buds, twigs, fruit, ferns, stems and roots of aquatic plants; in fall and winter, cuttings from trees stored underwater

Mating: December to January; gestation of 100-110 days

Den: lodge, usually on a lake or riverbank; dome-shaped structure, 2-10' tall, 12-14' wide, with underwater entrance

Young: 1-4 kits born with thick dark fur; 1 lb. each; able to swim soon after birth; nurse for 8-10 weeks; fully independent at 2 years

Predators: coyote and bobcat

Tracks: often erased by tail as it drags behind

Description: The beaver is a large rodent with prominent large teeth and a large, flat, paddle-shaped tail. Look for cuttings near the shoreline and mud mounds marked with scent. Listen for tail slaps on the water.

mammals

6"

DID YOU KNOW...? Found only in North America, and most common wildcat here, the bobcat is named for stubby, bobbed tail. It can leap 7-10' in a single bound. excellent climber, it uses trees for resting, observation a protection. It can travel 3-7 miles for a hunt and sto uneaten food under vegetation.

nocturnal   crepuscular

BOBCAT
Lynx rufus

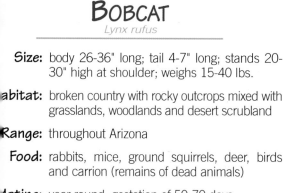

Size: body 26-36" long; tail 4-7" long; stands 20-30" high at shoulder; weighs 15-40 lbs.

Habitat: broken country with rocky outcrops mixed with grasslands, woodlands and desert scrubland

Range: throughout Arizona

Food: rabbits, mice, ground squirrels, deer, birds and carrion (remains of dead animals)

Mating: year-round; gestation of 50-70 days

Den: located in hollow logs, on rocky ledges and in caves and thickets; some make dens in abandoned or little-used barns and buildings

Young: 2-3 kittens born blind; 10" long; 12 oz. each; eyes open a few days after birth; nurse for 8 weeks; begin to eat meat at 4 weeks; fully independent at 5 months

Predators: coyote; Great Horned Owl and mountain lion prey on young

Tracks: large, cat-like with 4 toes and a larger rear pad

Description: The bobcat has a yellowish gray coat with red-brown streaks and a sprinkling of black and a soft beige underside. It is mostly gray during winter months. Signs may include scratch marks on trees and shredded bark.

2"

mammals

DID YOU KNOW...? The desert cottontail is one of 14 su species of cottontails. It is named for its cotton-like tail and famous naturalist John James Audubon as indicated by species name *audubonii*. Although the desert cottontail capable of reaching speeds of 20 mph, it often evades pre tors by lying motionless for extended periods of time. Like cottontails, it is coprophagous, which means it consum its feces to obtain any remaining nutrients.

nocturnal   crepuscular

COTTONTAIL, DESERT
Sylvilagus audubonii

Size: body 12-15" long; weighs 2-3 lbs.

Habitat: desert and arid shrub land in heaviest available brush

Range: throughout Arizona

Food: grasses, cacti, shrubs and bark; water obtained from food

Mating: year-round in some areas; 8 months per year in other areas; gestation of 28 days

Den: rests in forms (depressions on the ground); bears young in fur-lined abandoned burrows or forms

Young: 2 or more litters per year; 2-4 kittens born hairless and blind; 4" long; 1 oz. each; eyes open at 1 week; weaned at 2 weeks; independent at 4 weeks; reach sexual maturity at 80 days

Predators: raptors (birds of prey), fox, coyote and bobcat; some snakes prey on young

Tracks: 3" hind

Description: The desert cottontail has tan to gray fur with overall yellowish tinge and an orange scruff and throat [patch]. Its prominent ears have a slight hair covering and the blood vessels located near the surface of the skin, which help to dissipate heat. The female is larger than the male. The average lifespan is 2 years.

1½"

3"

mammals

DID YOU KNOW...? Known as the trickster in certain Nat
American folklore because of its clever ways, the coyote
unique to North America. It's capable of running at speeds
more than 30 mph. Its distinct howl, coupled with short hig
pitched yelps can often be heard in rural areas, sometimes
far away as 3 miles. Coyotes are sometimes spotted in sub
ban areas.

diurnal   crepuscular

COYOTE
Canis latrans

Size: body 32-40" long; tail 12-15" long; stands 15-20" high at shoulder; weighs 18-40 lbs.

Habitat: broken country, woodlands, grasslands and deserts

Range: throughout Arizona

Food: mice, squirrels, rabbits and other small mammals, birds, snakes, sometimes pronghorn, deer and carrion (remains of dead animals); stores uneaten food under leaves and soil

Mating: January to April; gestation of 58-63 days

Den: in roots of old trees, on hillsides, in gravel pits, in wooded thickets, under hollow logs, or in a bank along the water's edge

Young: 5-10 pups born blind and grayish; 8 oz. each; eyes open at 8-14 days; nurse for several weeks; later both adults feed pups regurgitated food; independent at 6-9 months

Predators: wolf; Great Horned Owl, Golden Eagle and mountain lion may take pups

Tracks: similar to medium-sized dog tracks with 4 toes and a rear pad

Description: Coyotes are light brown to gray with reddish, pale undersides and a bushy black-tipped tail.

2½"

mammals

male

DID YOU KNOW...? The mule deer, commonly called mule has tremendous eyesight and hearing, which help it to avo predators. It has several glands that secrete scent (pheromone to communicate territory, danger and mating readiness. Li most hoofed animals, its stomach has four distinct compa ments that help it to digest tough woody plants. Furth digestion occurs as the mule deer chews its cud (pre ously consumed food brought up for further chewing

crepuscular

DEER, MULE
Odocoileus hemionus

Size: body 6' long; 3½' at the shoulder; weighs 125-200 lbs.

abitat: mountainous forests and deserts

Range: throughout Arizona

Food: juniper, sagebrush, buckbrush and cliffrose

Mating: October to February; gestation of 6½ months

edding Site: often "bed down" on high, brushy ground usually near forest edge

Young: twin fawns are born covered with spots; 5-11 lbs. each; stand and nurse within hours of birth; nurse for about 6 weeks; fully independent at 1-2 years

lators: mountain lion, wolf and jaguar; coyote, black bear and bobcat may take fawns

Tracks: two crescent-shaped halves creating a heart-shaped track 2-4" long

cription: The mule deer is named for its prominent, -like ears that measure 9" in length. It is brownish gray lighter undersides and rump. Its tail is tipped with . In spring, males grow very large, bony antlers that are in winter.

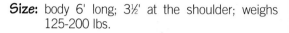

mammals 2"

DID YOU KNOW...? When alarmed, the white-tailed de raises its tail resembling a white flag. It can run up to 35-40 m During the breeding season, males make scrape marks sapling trees with their antlers to make rival males aware of th presence. Males spar with each other over females. Arizona home to the Coues deer, a unique subspecies of the white-tail deer. They are smaller than other white-tailed deer.

crepuscular

DEER, WHITE-TAILED
Odocoileus virginianus couesii

Size: body 4-6' long; tail 6-13" long; stands 2-3' high at shoulder; weighs 65-100 lbs.

Habitat: wooded, overgrown or brushy areas to sleep; feed in open fields

Range: central, east central and southeastern Arizona

Food: in summer, mushrooms, wildflowers and crops; in winter, acorns and bark from willow, oak and maple trees

Mating: December to March; gestation of 7 months; males make scrapes, which are patches of muddy ground where they urinate to attract females

Bedding Site: shallow depressions in hidden, grassy areas

Young: 1 or 2 fawns born with white spots for camouflage; 8 lbs. each; spots remain for 3-4 months; nurse for several months; males independent at 1 year, females at 2 years

Predators: mountain lion; bobcat, coyote and eagle prey upon fawns

Tracks: narrow, heart-shaped with split hoof

Description: White-tailed deer have a reddish brown in summer, grayish brown in winter. In spring, males forward-facing antlers that are shed in winter.

mammals

3"

DID YOU KNOW...? Before European settlers arrived in No America, there were approximately 10 million elk. By the ea 1900s, however, the elk population had dropped significan Today, thanks to conservation efforts, the elk population h grown to nearly 1 million. Elk can run 30-40 mph.

crepuscular

ELK
Cervus elaphus

Size: body 5-8' long; tail 3-8" long; stands 3-5' at shoulder; weighs 450-1,200 lbs.

Habitat: open woodlands

Range: north central and east central Arizona

Food: grass, buds, herbs and mushrooms in summer; twigs, bark and grass beneath snow in winter

Mating: September to October; gestation of 8 months

Bedding Site: hidden grassy or forested areas

Young: one calf born tan, speckled with white spots; 35 lbs; able to stand shortly after birth; females form nursery groups to care for calves; young join herd at 16 days; nurse for 60 days; develop adult color at 60 days

Predators: mountain lion, bear, wolf and coyote prey on calves

Tracks: heart-shaped, similar to white-tailed deer

Description: Usually found in remote wooded areas, the elk is dark brown to reddish brown with a yellowish rump patch. Males grow antlers that can measure up to 5' across.

mammals

4½"

DID YOU KNOW...? The gray fox is also known as the tr[ee] fox. It is the only member of the canine family (foxes, coyot[es,] wolves) capable of climbing trees. Even young pups can clin[b] trees. The gray fox uses its front legs to grasp the tree and [its] hind legs to push upward. Trees provide refuge from predato[rs] and sometimes food, including birds and bird eggs. The gr[ay] fox can reach speeds of 26-29 mph for short distance[s.]

☾ *nocturnal*   ☀ *crepuscular*

FOX, GRAY
Urocyon cinereoargenteus

Size: body 21-45" long; tail 11-16" long; stands 14" high at shoulder; weighs 7-13 lbs.

Habitat: arid rocky areas, desert and chaparral and canyon country

Range: throughout Arizona

Food: birds, bird eggs, rabbits, reptiles, berries and fruit

Mating: December to March; gestation of 51-63 days

Den: abandoned burrows, rock outcrops, caves and hollow trees; lined with vegetation; may have multiple chambers

Young: 1 litter per year; 3-7 dark brown pups born blind; 3½ ounces each; eyes open 9-12 days; weaned at 8-10 weeks; male helps care for the young

Predators: mountain lion, wolf, coyote, domestic dog and eagle

Tracks: small, dog-like prints show four toes and nails

Description: The fur of the gray fox is gray and tipped with . Its sides and neck are reddish and its undersides are . It has large, pointed ears, short legs and a furry tail d with black.

1½"

DID YOU KNOW...? The black-tailed jackrabbit is actuall hare since it does not build a nest for its young. It inhabits four deserts of the southwest including the Chihuahu. Mohave, Sonoran and Great Basin. As a prey species, black-tailed jackrabbit relies heavily on its protective color for camouflage, which allows it to blend in with its surrou ings and helps to conceal it from predators.

(nocturnal   crepuscular

JACKRABBIT, BLACK-TAILED
Lepus californicus

Size: body 17-25" long; ears 6-7" long; weighs 5-8 lbs.

Habitat: most environments; prefers open shrub land and desert

Range: throughout Arizona

Food: mesquite leaves and beans; buds, twigs and bark; grasses, forbs

Mating: year-round; peak December to September; gestation of 41-47 days

Den: no den or burrow constructed; use forms (shallow, bowl-shaped depressions on the ground) usually near cover (e.g., brush or vegetation)

Young: 3-4 litters per year; usually 2 young per litter; precocial (born fully mobile, covered with fur and able to see); 2 oz. each; weaned at about 4 weeks; fully grown by 8 months

Predators: coyote, bobcat, fox, hawk, eagle, snake and owl

Tracks: indistinct because of hair on bottoms of feet; hind print is larger than front

Description: The fur of the black-tailed jackrabbit is buff to brownish gray and tipped with black. It has lighter under-parts and black-tipped ears and tail. It has long hind legs, long ears and large, furry feet. The female is larger than the male.

1½"

2½"

mammals

DID YOU KNOW...? The javelina is the only pig-like spec native to North America, but it is not a true pig. It has a ke sense of smell, which it uses to find underground bulbs a roots. The name javelina is Spanish for spear referring to tusks. It is also known as tayaussa, musk hog and colla peccary. The typical herd size is 8-12. Arizona has a large p ulation numbering roughly 60,000 animals.

🌙 *nocturnal*   ☀ *crepuscular*

JAVELINA
Pecari tajacu

Size: body 29-39" long; tail 2" long; stands 17-23" high at shoulder; weighs 35-60 lbs.

Habitat: desert and arid woodlands

Range: central and southern Arizona; isolated populations in western Arizona

Food: flowers, fruits, nuts, cacti, bulbs, roots, grubs and reptiles

Mating: year-round, peak during January to March; gestation of 140-145 days

Den: caves, hollow logs, abandoned burrows and thickets

Young: 1-4 young born fully mobile; reddish brown to yellow with dark dorsal stripe; 1 lb. each; weaned at 6-8 weeks; independent in 2-3 months; 1-2 litters per year

Predators: black bear, mountain lion, bobcat and jaguar; coyote and eagle prey on young

Tracks: heart-shaped hooves; 1-1½" long

Description: The javelina is dark gray with a white collar circling its neck. The male has spear-like tusks that measure 1" in length. The average lifespan is 7-8 years.

1½"

mammals

female with cubs

DID YOU KNOW...? The mountain lion is the second-large member of the cat family inhabiting North America (only t jaguar is larger). The mountain lion is known by several nam including cougar, puma, panther and catamount (cat of t mountains). Although it is capable of reaching speeds of . mph for short distances, it commonly ambushes its pr Leaping 15' in a single bound, the mountain lion kills . prey by breaking its neck or back. It has a hor range of 75-200 square miles.

nocturnal   *crepuscular*

LION, MOUNTAIN
Puma concolor

Size: body 6-8' long; tail 2-3' long; weighs 75-200 lbs.

Habitat: mountains, foothills, canyons, swamps, open woodlands, forests and deserts

Range: throughout Arizona

Food: mule deer, white-tailed deer, bighorn sheep, rabbits and javelina

Mating: breeds year-round; gestation of 14 weeks; mate every other year

Den: cave, cliffside ledge, sheltered rock outcrop or under fallen log

Young: 1-4 cubs born blind with spotted fur; weigh 1 lb. each; eyes soon open, colored blue which later changes to brown; cubs nurse for 8-12 weeks; independent at 1¼-2 years

Predators: hawk, owl, black bear and adult male mountain lions may take young

Tracks: front foot has 5 toes but only 4 make up the track; hind foot 4 toes slightly smaller; up to 3" long and 4" wide

Description: The mountain lion is grayish brown to tawny with lighter undersides and a long tail tipped with black. Its excellent eyesight allowing it to hunt in the dark. Large padded feet allow the cougar to stalk its prey virtually undetected.

mammals

3"

DID YOU KNOW...? The muskrat creates a V-shaped wa as it swims. It can hold its breath underwater for up to 15 m utes. This skill is important as the muskrat works with catta grass and mud to build lodges in the water. The lodges me sure up to 2' high and 4' across and a good lodge can be us by several generations for 20 or 30 years.

crepuscular

MUSKRAT
Ondatra zibethicus

Size: body 9-13" long; tail 7-12" long; weighs 2-4 lbs.

Habitat: marshes, ponds, rivers, streams and lakes with thick vegetation

Range: throughout Arizona except in southeast and northeast

Food: cattails, fish, frogs, crayfish, snails and apples

Mating: February to September; gestation of 25-30 days

Den: underground along the water's edge, or lodges built on platforms

Young: 2-3 litters per year; 1-11 young born blind; ¾ oz. each; eyes open at 14-18 days; nurse for 3-4 weeks; independent at 4 weeks

Predators: fox, coyote, hawk and owl

Tracks: although they have 5 toes on each foot, only 4 show clear imprint; hind feet partly webbed

Description: The muskrat is a dark reddish brown to black animal with slightly lighter undersides and a long, rat-like, mostly hairless tail. In winter, muskrats gnaw a hole in the ice and push vegetation up through it. These are called push-ups and are used as feeding sites.

1¼"

2"

DID YOU KNOW...? The otter's torpedo-shaped body allo it to glide effortlessly through the water. Otters can tread wa and swim on their fronts, backs and sides. It is able to div depths of 50' and hold its breath for 6-8 minutes at a tin The otter uses slides or shoreline chutes into the water, a makes otter rolls, which are bowl-shaped areas 20-100' fr the water where it dries off and marks territory.

crepuscular

OTTER, RIVER
Lontra canadensis

Size: body 18-32" long; tail 11-20" long; weighs 10-30 lbs.

Habitat: lakes, rivers and streams

Range: currently limited to central Arizona waterways

Food: fish, minnows, frogs, mussels, snakes, crayfish and turtles

Mating: December to April; gestation of 60-63 days (after a delayed period of 9-10 months after mating)

Den: near water; lined with plant material; may use upturned logs or stumps, muskrat or beaver lodges

Young: 1-5 pups born blind and fur covered; 5 oz. each; eyes open at 1 month; explore outside the den at 2 months; continue to nurse for 4 months; fully independent at 6 months

Predators: mountain lion

Tracks: often hidden by dragging tail; front and hind feet show 5 toes

Description: The otter is long and sleek with a muscular tail and dark brown coat. Well-adapted to life in and under the water, it has a layer of insulating fat, dense fur, webbed feet, and ear and nose flaps.

3"

mammals

DID YOU KNOW...? Approximately 30,000 quills provide t̶ common porcupine with a unique defense. When confront̶ by a would-be attacker, it swats the animal (or person) with tail, which is loaded with needle-sharp 4" quills. It does ̶ shoot its quills. Barbed ends cause the quills to work their w̶ deeper into the attacker's muscles, making them difficult a̶ painful to extract.

nocturnal

PORCUPINE
Erethizon dorsatum

Size: body 18-23" long; tail 6-12" long; weighs 10-28 lbs.

Habitat: many environments; main requirement is woody vegetation

Range: throughout Arizona except southwest quarter

Food: clover, grass, seeds, corn, leaves and evergreen needles, aquatic plants, acorns, bark and twigs

Mating: September to December; gestation of 200-217 days

Den: hollow logs, tree cavities, under stumps and buildings, in caves and in the abandoned burrows of other animals

Young: a single pup born with dark fur and soft 1" quills; 1 lb.; nurses for 3 months; fully independent at 5 months

Predators: Great Horned Owl

Tracks: show long nails and bumpy pads; often hidden by dragging tail

Description: The porcupine is a large, round-bodied animal. It has color variations that include dark gray, dark brown and black, with thousands of cactus-like quills. They spend the day resting in trees.

2⅝"

3⅜"

mammals

DID YOU KNOW...? The pronghorn is very unique for sever reasons: 1) it is the fastest land mammal in North America, 2 is found nowhere else in the world, 3) it is the only mammal w branched horns, 4) it is the only mammal to shed its horns, a 5) it is the sole surviving member of its family. The pronghe has tremendous eyesight and is capable of seeing movem several miles away. Known as the prairie ghost, the pro horn can reach sustained speeds of 35-60 mph, wh is important, since speed is its primary defense.

diurnal   crepuscular

PRONGHORN
Antilocapra americana

Size: body 4-4½' long; stands 3-3½' at shoulder; weighs 70-140 lbs.

Habitat: semiarid prairies, basins, rangeland and plains

Range: throughout Arizona

Food: sagebrush, forbs, grasses, clover, lupine, cacti and cedar

Mating: August to September

Bedding Site: dense areas of sagebrush and grasses; may rest in the open for short periods

Young: twins are common; young (called kid) are born virtually odorless; 5-9 lbs. each; can remain motionless for hours as concealment, but 50% of all young are lost to predators; independent by fall

Predators: coyote, fox, mountain lion, eagle and sometimes bobcat prey on young

Tracks: front 3½" long; hind 2½" long; blocky, heart-shaped hooves

Description: The pronghorn is cinnamon brown with white sides, white stripes on its neck and a distinct white patch, which serves to warn other pronghorn. Its prog eyes provide it with excellent peripheral vision. Both have simple black horns that are covered in an outer h. Males' horns measure 6-19" in length, and es' horns are only about 4" long.

3"

mammals

DID YOU KNOW...? The raccoon is an excellent climber and swimmer. Contrary to popular belief, it does not wash every thing it eats. Clever and agile, the raccoon is highly adapted gathering and eating a great variety of foods. In the fall develops a thick layer of fat.

nocturnal

Zzz partial
hibernator

RACCOON
Procyon lotor

Size: body 16-28" long; tail 8-12" long; stands 12" high at shoulder; weighs 15-40 lbs.

Habitat: wooded areas near meadows, rivers and ponds

Range: throughout Arizona except in south central area

Food: nuts, berries, insects, crayfish, garden vegetables, grain, rodents, carrion (remains of dead animals) and garbage

Mating: December to January; gestation of 63 days

Den: found in hollow trees, woodchuck burrows, culverts and under buildings

Young: 2-7 young born blind, with a light fur covering, a faint mask, and ringed tail; 4" long; 2 oz. each; eyes open at 21 days; nurse for several weeks; leave den at 10 weeks; fully independent at 4-6 months

Predators: coyote, fox, bobcat, Great Horned Owl and domestic dog

Tracks: small, hand-like prints

Description: The raccoon has heavy fur streaked brown, and gray with a distinctive black face mask and a , ringed tail. They are commonly seen raiding ge cans and getting into other mischief. They spend daytime sunbathing in trees.

3"

mammals

DID YOU KNOW...? The ringtail is named for its promin[...] raccoon-like tail. It is also known as miner's cat, civet cat a[...] cacomistle, an Aztec Nahuatl word, which means half mo[...] tain lion. An agile climber, the ringtail uses its long tail [...] balance as it ricochets back and forth between narrow r[...] crevices. The ringtail was named the Arizona State Mamm[...] in 1986.

nocturnal

RINGTAIL

Bassariscus astutus

Size: body 14-17" long; tail 19" long; weighs 30-45 oz.

Habitat: rocky areas of canyons and peaks, abandoned mines; usually near water

Range: throughout Arizona

Food: birds, lizards, small mammals, insects, cactus fruits and other plants

Mating: February to May; gestation of 45-50 days

Den: abandoned burrows, rocky outcrops and hollow logs; lined with vegetation

Young: 1 litter per year; 2-4 young born blind with a fine coating of hair; less than 1 oz. each; eyes open at 31-34 days; weaned at 4 months

Predators: bobcat, coyote, Great Horned Owl and fox; sometimes raccoon

Tracks: nonretractable claws; catlike tracks

Description: The fur of the ringtail is gray to buff and tipped with black. Its undersides are lighter. It has a dark mask area and large ears that are edged with white. It has an exceptionally long tail with multiple dark rings.

1"

mammals

male

female

DID YOU KNOW...? Crack! The sound of crashing horns synonymous with bighorn sheep. Males battle for breed rights by ramming heads at speeds of 20 mph. This continu until one of them backs down. The skull of the bighorn she has a special skeletal structure that serves to absorb impact of the head-on collision. The bottoms of a bigh sheep's hooves have a spongy texture that allows it to g steep mountainsides and climb and jump with ease

diurnal

SHEEP, DESERT BIGHORN
Ovis canadensis mexicana

Size: body 4-4½' long; stands 2½-3½' at shoulder; weighs 75-225 lbs.

abitat: desert mountain ranges

Range: throughout Arizona except in east central area

Food: mesquite, ironwood, jojoba and grasses; water requirements are mostly met by foods such as cacti

Mating: July to September; gestation of 5-6 months

t Site: none constructed

Young: twins are rare; 8-10 lbs.; dark gray; only 1/3 survive to adulthood; born in February

ators: mountain lion, bobcat, sometimes bear and coyote; eagles prey on young

Tracks: wedge-shaped and blocky with rounded tips

ription: The desert bighorn sheep is dark grayish to cream with a white muzzle and rump patch and -tipped tail. The male has flat, wide spreading horns weigh up to 30 lbs. and measure up to 33" in length 15" in circumference. The female has smaller horns. horns are never shed; new growth occurs each year. na is home to two subspecies of bighorn sheep: *Ovis densis nelsoni* and *O. c. mexicana*. They can be part by subtle differences between their horns.

DID YOU KNOW...? The skunk is famous for defending its with a foul-smelling spray it squirts up to 15'. Even a 3-week old kit can spray! Before spraying, a skunk usually hiss stomps its front feet and waves its tail in warning. Althou skunks are blamed for those smells along woods, fields a trails, fox and coyote mark their territories with a strong mus scent very similar to that of a skunk.

(nocturnal   Zzz *partial hibernator*

SKUNK, STRIPED
Mephitis mephitis

Size: body 15" long; tail 7-8" long; weighs 3-10 lbs.

Habitat: rocky areas or ravines with thick vegetation; prefer to be near water

Range: throughout Arizona

Food: mice, insects, fruit, eggs and garbage

Mating: February to March; gestation of 60-70 days

Den: abandoned badger or fox dens or enlarged ground squirrel or gopher burrows

Young: 5-9 kits born in April-May, blind, wrinkled and toothless; 7 oz. each; their short hair shows the distinctive color pattern; eyes open at 3 weeks; weaned at 8 weeks; independent at 10 weeks

Predators: Great Horned Owl, bobcat, mountain lion, coyote and fox

Tracks: shows five toes across each foot

Description: The striped skunk has a glossy black coat a thin white stripe between the eyes and a broad white shaped stripe on its back and down its bushy tail.

1"

DID YOU KNOW...? The round-tailed ground squirrel live colony-like social groups, which provide some protect against predators. It uses vocalization as a means of alarm warn of approaching danger. A shrill whistle is associated aerial predators and a loud chatter is associated with la predators. The round-tailed ground squirrel retreats to its b row in extreme weather and enters a torpor state becom inactive or dormant for an extended period during win

diurnal   Zzz *partial hibernator*

SQUIRREL, ROUND-TAILED GROUND
Spermophilus tereticaudus

Size: body 6" long; tail 2-4" long; weighs 4-6 oz.

Habitat: desert with creosote and saltbush or arid shrub land

Range: western, central and southern Arizona

Food: seeds, grasses, nuts, bulbs, insects and bird eggs; water obtained from food

Mating: January to March; gestation 25-35 days

Den: multi-chambered burrow with several entrances; grass-lined

Young: 1 litter per year; 4-9 born blind and hairless; less than 1 oz. each; nurse 4-6 weeks; fully grown in 25 days; sexually mature at 10-11 months

Predators: snake, fox, coyote, bobcat, raptors (birds of prey) and domestic cat

Tracks: small tracks show four toes on the front feet and five on the hind

Description: The round-tailed ground squirrel is brown to grayish gray with lighter undersides. It has a short, furry short legs and broad furry feet.

1"

DID YOU KNOW...? The Mexican gray wolf is also known the Spanish word lobo. Government-sponsored predator control programs of the late 1800s and mid 1900s led to elimination in the wild. It was listed as endangered by the United States Fish and Wildlife Service (USFWS) in 1976. Arizona, the last known animal was taken in 1970. In 199 the USFWS, in cooperation with the Arizona Game a Fish Department, released Mexican gray wolves in the Apache National Forest in eastern Arizona.

diurnal

WOLF, MEXICAN GRAY
Canis lupus baileyi

Size: body 40-52" long; tail 13-19" long; stands 26-32" high at shoulder; weighs 60-80 lbs.

abitat: coniferous and pine-oak forests

Range: reintroduced over most of east central Arizona in the Apache-Sitgreaves National Forest and Gila National Forest (Blue Range Wolf Recovery Area)

Food: deer, elk, birds, rabbits and other small mammals; pack members hunt together

Mating: February to March; gestation of 63 days

Den: usually dug by pregnant female; found in hollow logs, rocky outcrops, or in hillside burrows; used for 8-10 weeks

Young: 4-6 pups born blind with a dark coat; 1 lb. each; eyes open at 2 weeks; nurse for 6-8 weeks; fed regurgitated meat and cared for by pack members; begin to hunt with pack at 6 months; fully grown at 1 year

dators: no natural predators

Tracks: similar to large dog with 4 toes and 1 rear pad

cription: The Mexican gray wolf is the smallest sub-ies of gray wolf. Its coat is buff to gray with black and tones. It lives and hunts in packs of 6-12 members.

4"

mammals

DID YOU KNOW...? The white-throated woodrat is also kno as the trade rat or pack rat for its habit of collecting and hoa ing shiny objects. Its large, elaborate midden provides she from the extreme temperatures of the desert. The midd which is made partly of cactus spines, also helps protect woodrat from predators.

nocturnal

WOODRAT, WHITE-THROATED
Neotoma albigula

Size: body 7-8" long; tail 5-7" long; weighs 6.9-16 oz.

Habitat: desert, dry plains and pinyon-juniper forests

Range: throughout Arizona except in extreme north-west

Food: seeds, fruits, leaves, berries, cacti, grasses and insects; water obtained from food

Mating: year-round with a decline from August to October; gestation of 30-40 days

Nest: large, dome-shaped midden (heap of sticks and vegetation, including cactus spines); often located in clumps of cacti, creosote or mesquite trees; more than one entrance; lined with vegetation

Young: 2-3 litters per year; 2-4 young born blind; less than 1 oz. each; eyes open at 15-21 days; weaned at 4 weeks

Predators: coyote, fox, snake, owl, hawk, ringtail and domestic cat

Tracks: show four toes and multiple pads

Description: The white-throated woodrat is gray with white undersides. It has white feet and a bicolored tail of white and gray.

mammals

¾"

DID YOU KNOW...? Male and female Red-winged Blackbir[ds] do not migrate together. The males return to the breeding ar[ea] several weeks before the females. The male establishes a[nd] defends a nesting site to attract one or more females. While t[ry]ing to attract a mate, males can puff up their colorful epaule[ts] to gain more attention. During migration, they often flock w[ith] other species of blackbirds, such as grackles and cowbirds

BLACKBIRD, RED-WINGED
Agelaius phoeniceus

Size: body 7½-9½" long; 10-13" wingspan; 1.8 oz.

Habitat: wetlands and grasslands

Range: throughout Arizona

Food: seeds and insects

Mating: early spring

Nest: bowl-shaped; attached to marsh reeds about 12" above water; cattails provide protection from weather and predators

Eggs: average clutch 3-5; pale blue marked with purple and black spots and streaks; 2-3 broods per year

Young: hatch blind and featherless in 11 days; females tend the eggs; males defend the nest; eyes open at 1 week; flight feathers develop at 10 days; young leave nesting area at 20 days

Predators: Sharp-shinned Hawk, Cooper's Hawk, Merlin (winter only) and Great Horned Owl; raccoon and skunk prey on eggs and nestlings

Migration: present year-round; winter population increases due to migrants from the north

Description: Males are black with bright red and gold epaulets (wing patches) and the females are streaked brown-and-white.

birds

DID YOU KNOW...? In general, male birds have brigh' more colorful plumage than females. Bright coloring serves attract females and distract predators, while drab coloring p vides beneficial camouflage for nesting. Camouflage is protective adaptation that allows a bird to disguise itself blend in with its surroundings.

BLUEBIRD, MOUNTAIN
Sialia currucoides

Size: body 6-7½" long; 14" wingspan; 1 oz.

Habitat: mountain woodlands and rangeland

Range: east central and northern Arizona

Food: insects; occasional fruit and seeds

Mating: early spring

Nest: cavity nest; woodpecker holes, cliffside crevices and artificial structures; lined with grasses

Eggs: average clutch 4-6; pale blue; 2 broods common

Young: young hatch blind and featherless in 12-14 days; eyes open at approximately 1 week; flight feathers develop at 15-18 days

Predators: Cooper's Hawk, Sharp-shinned Hawk, Merlin (winter only), Northern Goshawk and Great Horned Owl; raccoon preys on eggs and nestlings

Migration: present year-round; wanders throughout Arizona in winter

Description: The male is bright sky-blue with lighter under-. The female is brownish gray with lighter undersides.

soaring

DID YOU KNOW...? California Condor populations dropp[ed] drastically due to habitat loss, slow reproduction, collisi[on] with power lines and lead poisoning from consuming carri[on] containing lead shot. By 1985, 9 condors were left in the w[ild.] USFWS biologists captured and tagged them for placement [in] a captive-breeding program. In 1996, six condors were re[in]troduced to Arizona's Vermillion Cliffs. Today, though [still] endangered, there are 157 California Condors, some of wh[ich] can be seen soaring high over Arizona's canyon country.

CONDOR, CALIFORNIA
Gymnogyps californianus

Size: body 46" long; 9' wingspan; 16-23 lbs.

Habitat: cliffsides and mountainous terrain

Range: northern Arizona

Food: carrion (remains of dead animals); cleans feathers after feeding

Mating: December to May; pairs mate for life; breed once every 2 years

Nest: ground nest in caves and on cliffsides

Eggs: average clutch 1; white; a second egg will be laid if the first is broken

Young: hatch in 50-56 days; leave the nest at 6 months; both the male and female help care for the young which is fully dependent upon them for up to one year; young reach sexual maturity at 5-6 years

Predators: eagle, bobcat and mountain lion; adult condors may prey on other chicks

Migration: present year-round

Description: The California Condor is the largest land bird in North America. It is dull gray-black with a patch of white under its wings. Its neck and head are bare and bright reddish orange. The condor is capable of flight speeds of 55 mph and soars at altitudes of 15,000 feet.

birds

DID YOU KNOW...? The American Coot is commo͏
referred to as the mudhen. It feeds throughout the day, div͏
for aquatic plants and skimming the surface for insects͏
avoids predators by running across the water. They produ͏
many young.

COOT, AMERICAN
Fulica americana

Size: body 13-17" long; weighs 1-1½ lbs.

Habitat: wetlands

Range: throughout Arizona

Food: aquatic plants, grass, insects, small fish and tadpoles

Mating: April to May

Nest: cup-shaped; nests float hidden among cattails

Eggs: average clutch 8-12; buff with black spots; 1 brood per year

Young: hatch in 21-22 days; have reddish orange down; males and females care for young; leave nest 1-2 days after hatching but remain with adults for 7 weeks

Predators: Bald Eagle, hawk, owl; raccoon preys on eggs and nestlings

Duration: present year-round

Description: Often seen in large flocks, this dark gray bird has a black head and white bill with a red ring near the tip. It also has prominent red eyes and a red patch on the bill between the eyes. Its feet are lobed and olive green. It has short wings and tail. Its 3-toed lobed feet create distinct tracks along the shoreline.

DID YOU KNOW...? The majority of the Sandhill Cranes t[hat] winter in Arizona–about 20,000–spend their time in the sou[th] eastern part of the state near the Wilcox Playa. Sand[hill] Cranes that spend the winter in Arizona come from three [dis-] tinct populations. The Sandhill Crane travels up to 300 m[iles] a day during its migration. In the spring, males and fema[les] perform an elaborate courtship display that involves singi[ng,] bowing, skipping and leaping as high as 15-20' into the ai[r.]

CRANE, SANDHILL
Grus canadensis

Size: body 4' long; 6½' wingspan; 6-12 lbs.

Habitat: wetland areas usually near open fields

Range: southeast and south central Arizona

Food: omnivorous ground feeders; insects, small mammals, amphibians, reptiles, bulbs, seeds and waste grain

Mating: March and May; male and female return to the same nesting site each spring

Nest: constructed out of plant material and located on the ground near water

Eggs: average clutch 2; large, drab olive to buff spotted with brown; 1 brood per year

Young: hatch in 28-32 days covered with down and able to feed themselves; able to fly at 2-3 months; fully independent at about 1 year

Predators: bobcat, coyote and Bald Eagle; fox prey on eggs

Migration: present as a winter visitor when small numbers migrate from the north into Arizona

Description: The Sandhill Crane is gray with a dark red on its head and red eyes. Sometimes its plumage appears to be rusty brown because of staining. It has a long neck, beak and legs. It forages for food within the range of 3-35 square miles.

birds

DID YOU KNOW...? The Mourning Dove is named for its sa sounding coo. The pigeon milk (regurgitated liquid) it provid its young is more nutritious than cow's milk. It is the me abundant and widespread dove in the U.S. Huge flocks gath in farm fields to feed on fallen grain. It is able to reach flig speeds of 60 mph.

DOVE, MOURNING
Zenaida macroura

Size: 10-12" long; 18" wingspan; 3-6 oz.

Habitat: open wooded areas, marshes, orchards, roadsides, grasslands and farmland

Range: throughout Arizona

Food: seeds and grains

Mating: March to September

Nest: loosely constructed of twigs; found in trees, shrubs or on the ground

Eggs: average clutch of 2; white, unmarked eggs; 2-3 broods per year

Young: hatch blind and featherless in 13-14 days; eyes open at 1 week; feathers develop within 10 days; the male and female provide the young with pigeon milk (regurgitated liquid); leave the nest at 12-14 days

Predators: hawk, owl and domestic cat; squirrel and Greater Roadrunner prey on eggs and nestlings

Migration: present year-round

Description: The Mourning Dove is grayish brown with pinkish brown head, chest and undersides. It has a blue ring around its eye, a black bill, red legs and a long pointed tail edged with white.

birds

soaring

DID YOU KNOW...? Unique to North America, the Bald E
was chosen as our nation's symbol in 1782, narrowly bea
out the Wild Turkey. A powerful raptor, the Bald Eagle cat
its prey with its razor-sharp talons by swooping down at sp
of 50 mph. It was placed on the Federal Endangered Spe
list in 1978 due to agricultural pesticide contamination. S
the pesticide DDT was banned, the Bald Eagle population
recovered but populations are still closely monitored.

EAGLE, BALD
Haliaeetus leucocephalus

Size: body 3-3½' long; 6½-8' wingspan; 8-14 lbs.

Habitat: forested areas near rivers and lakes

Range: central and west central Arizona

Food: fish, waterfowl, birds and carrion (remains of dead animals); regurgitates pellets of indigestible parts of prey

Mating: November to March; mated pairs return to the same nest site each spring

Nest: located in tall trees or on cliffsides

Eggs: average clutch 1-3; large, dull-white; 1 brood per year; male and female care for eggs

Young: eaglets hatch in 35 days covered with gray down; 4 oz. each; male and female care for young; by 10-12 weeks grow brown feathers flecked with white; develop adult coloration, including white head, at 4-5 years

Predators: no natural predators

Migration: present year-round in a few areas; some migrate into Arizona for the winter

Description: The Bald Eagle is a large dark brown bird with a white head and tail. Its eyes, feet and beak are bright yellow. Large flocks may gather at feeding grounds during spring or fall migrations. Southwestern subspecies is slightly smaller than the northern.

birds

DID YOU KNOW...? A strong bird of prey, the Peregrine Falcon swoops down on its prey at speeds approaching 2 mph. Peregrine comes from the word peregrinate which means to travel or wander. This falcon was placed on the Federal Endangered Species list in 1984 due to agricultural pesticide contamination which caused thinning of the eggshells. The Peregrine Falcon was removed from the list 1999 as a result of successful captive breeding programs and reintroduction efforts.

FALCON, PEREGRINE
Falco peregrinus

Size: body 16-20" long; 40-45" wingspan; 19-40 oz.

Habitat: cliffs and bluffs, usually near water

Range: throughout Arizona except in extreme south-west

Food: small birds, shorebirds and waterfowl; it regurgitates pellets containing the indigestible parts of their prey, including bones, feathers and hair

Mating: April to July

Nest: often constructed on cliffs, bridges and sky-scrapers

Eggs: average clutch 2-5; creamy white speckled with brown; 1 brood per year

Young: hatch in 28-29 days covered with white down; male and female care for young, feeding them mice and birds; develop feathers at 3 weeks; leave the nest at 6-9 weeks

Predators: Great Horned Owl and eagle

Migration: present year-round; some migrate into Arizona each fall

Description: The Peregrine Falcon is brownish gray to blue with a dark face mask and lighter undersides are streaked with black or brown.

birds

soaring

DID YOU KNOW...? The Cooper's Hawk is known as chicken hawk because of its tendency to prey on domestic po try. The population declined from the 1930s to the 1970s to pesticide contamination. Its numbers have increased in West in recent years because of stricter pesticide regulation

HAWK, COOPER'S
Accipiter cooperii

Size: body 14-20" long; 29-37" wingspan; 10-20 oz.

Habitat: open wooded areas, riparian areas

Range: throughout Arizona except extreme southwest

Food: birds, squirrels, chipmunks and other small mammals; regurgitates pellets of indigestible parts of prey

Mating: March to July

Nest: usually found in the crotch of a tree 20-50' above the ground; constructed of sticks and lined with shredded bark; adults often return to same nest site each year

Eggs: average clutch 3-5; greenish with brown markings; 1 brood per year

Young: hatch blind and featherless in 36 days; eyes open at 1 week; flight feathers develop at 13-20 days; female tends eggs but male helps care for young until they leave the nest at 30 days

Predators: Common Raven, Northern Goshawk and Great Horned Owl prey on young

Migration: present year-round; some move to non-breeding areas in winter

Description: The Cooper's Hawk is grayish blue with undersides and reddish bars. It has a black-ed head and three black tail stripes.

birds

DID YOU KNOW...? The Red-tail is a powerful raptor (bird prey). Its eyesight is many times greater than a human's, a it can see a small mouse or rat from hundreds of feet in air. Listen for its high-pitched screams. Watch as it circ above its prey, then dives down to snatch it with its sh talons. The hawk has a sharp, curved beak adapted for te ing its prey into pieces as it eats.

HAWK, RED-TAILED
Buteo jamaicensis

Size: body 19-26" long; 4-4½' wingspan; males 1½-2 lbs.; females 2-4 lbs.

Habitat: farmland, woodland, prairie and desert scrub

Range: throughout Arizona

Food: small mammals, rabbits, snakes, birds and insects; regurgitates pellets of indigestible parts of prey

Mating: February to June

Nest: 28-38" across; lined with shredded bark and fine twigs; returns to same nest site each year

Eggs: average clutch 1-4; plain white or bluish and speckled; 1 brood per year

Young: hatch in 28-32 days covered with white down; males and females tend young; young leave the nest at 6-7 weeks

Predators: Golden Eagle; jays prey on nestlings; harassed by crow

Migration: present year-round

Description: The Red-tail appears in a variety of colors buff to brown, with a patterned, streaked underside is sometimes faintly rusty red. A Red-tailed Hawk in western U.S. has a brown chin. It usually has a reddish tail and is often seen perched on telephone poles.

soaring

DID YOU KNOW...? Also known as sharpie, the Sha
shinned Hawk can be seen preying on small birds at backya
feeders. It is named for the thin, raised ridge located along
tarsus bone. The scientific name *Accipiter* means swift w
and *striatus* means striped.

HAWK, SHARP-SHINNED
Accipiter striatus

Size: body 11" long; 23" wingspan; 5 oz.

Habitat: high elevation evergreen forests, riparian areas

Range: throughout Arizona's mountains

Food: small birds (90% of diet); small mammals and insects

Mating: April to August

Nest: platform; usually constructed in coniferous trees

Eggs: average clutch 4-5; white or light blue with brown or purple blotches; 1 brood per year

Young: hatch blind and featherless in 35 days; eyes open at 1 week; feathers develop within 2 weeks; leave the nest at 24 days; male hunts for the female during incubation period

Predators: no natural predators

Duration: present year-round; winter population increases due to migrants from the north

Description: About the size of a robin, the Sharp-shinned is small in comparison to other hawks. It has a long, red tail with a squared end and short, rounded wings. It is blue-gray with a dark cap and forehead. Its undersides are lighter with pinkish barring. Like the Cooper's Hawk, the Sharp-shinned Hawk has red-orange eyes.

birds

DID YOU KNOW...? The Great Blue Heron is the largest and most common heron species. Often miscalled a crane, herons are commonly seen stalking their prey along tidal rivers, estuaries, and pond and lake shores. Their large 4-toed feet help distribute their weight in the same manner as snowshoes, preventing the heron from sinking in mudflats.

HERON, GREAT BLUE
Ardea herodias

Size: body 39-52" long; 6-7' wingspan; 6-12 lbs.

Habitat: shallow lakes, ponds, rivers and marshes

Range: throughout Arizona

Food: frogs, snails, crayfish, fish, mice and insects

Mating: March to July

Nest: 2-3' across; grouped in large rookeries (colonies) in tall trees along water's edge, nests are built of sticks and often are located more than 100' above the ground; nests are used year after year

Eggs: average clutch 3-7; pale blue-green eggs; 1 brood per year

Young: hatch featherless in 26-29 days; male and female care for young by regurgitating food into their mouths; young leave nest at 2-4 weeks

Predators: Great Horned Owl and Golden Eagle

Migration: present year-round

Description: The Great Blue Heron has a blue gray back lighter undersides. It has a white head with a black long neck, long stick-like dark legs, and a long dagger-like pale yellow bill. Often seen standing still along the 's edge, hunting for food.

birds

female

DID YOU KNOW...? Anna's Hummingbird is one of t
North American hummingbird species that does not migra
It consumes half of its body weight each day in food, whic
equivalent to the nectar from 1,000 flower blossoms. Ann
Hummingbird is native to the western coastal states but h
successfully spread east to Arizona. In fact, southeast
Arizona is home to more species of hummingbirds than an
where else in the U.S.

HUMMINGBIRD, ANNA'S

Calypte anna

Size: body 4" long; 5¼" wingspan; less than 1 ounce

Habitat: desert

Range: south central and southwestern Arizona

Food: flower nectar, sap and insects

Mating: November to August

Nest: tiny, cup-shaped nest constructed of plant down and spider webs; covered with lichen; female constructs nest; usually near water

Eggs: average clutch 2; white, pea-sized; 2 broods per year

Young: hatch blind and featherless in 14-18 days; eyes open at 5 days; feathers develop at 6 days; leave the nest at 18-21 days; remain together for short time after leaving the nest

Predators: domestic cat; shrike preys on young; Western Scrub Jay preys on eggs

Migration: present year-round; some birds migrate out of Arizona each summer and return in fall

Description: Anna's Hummingbird is one of North America's largest hummingbird species. The male is mostly green with a ruby-red crown, chin and throat. The female is green with gray undersides. Anna's Hummingbird beats its wings 45 times per second.

birds

female

male

DID YOU KNOW...? Often referred to as the Sparrow Haw the American Kestrel is the smallest falcon in North America has dark spots on the back of its neck which are sometim called false eyes. Some people believe that the false eyes fool t kestrel's predators into thinking the kestrel has seen it, so it mi give up its pursuit. It can fly at speeds of 39 mph and hover place while hunting. Its keen eyesight allows it to see a grassho per 100' away. Kestrels can even be seen in urban areas.

KESTREL, AMERICAN
Falco sparverius

Size: body 8-12" long; 20-24" wingspan; 3¾-5¾ oz.

abitat: forested edges of open areas, grasslands and agricultural areas; deserts

Range: throughout Arizona

Food: insects, rodents, birds and snakes; regurgitates pellets of indigestible parts of prey

Mating: late spring

Nest: located in natural cavities of trees or cliffs, also in nest boxes

Eggs: average clutch 3-5; buff with reddish brown spots; 1 brood per year

Young: males and females care for eggs; hatch blind and featherless in 29-31 days; eyes open at 1 week; reach adult weight at 2½ weeks; leave nest at 4 weeks

dators: Great Horned Owl and Cooper's Hawk

ration: present year-round

cription: The American Kestrel is often seen perching ires, fence posts, dead branches and utility poles near spaces. This small falcon has a rust colored back and and white chest, cheek and chin patches. Males have blue wings while females have reddish brown wings.

female

male

DID YOU KNOW...? The Mallard is the most abundant a[n]
widespread of all waterfowl species and can be found alm[o]
anywhere in the world. It is a dabbling duck (also called pu[d]
dle duck) and feeds with its tail straight up in the air or
skimming the water just below the surface. Like all ducks, t[he]
Mallard has a lamellate bill, which means it has tooth-li[ke]
edges that act much like a strainer allowing the duck to h[old]
a piece of food while the water drains through.

MALLARD
Anas platyrhynchos

Size: 20-23" long; 36" wingspan; 1-2¾ lbs.

Habitat: lakes, ponds, rivers and swamps

Range: northern, central and eastern Arizona

Food: aquatic plants, aquatic insects, grasses, seeds and grains

Mating: April to July; mating pairs are formed each fall

Nest: ground nest; bowl-shaped, 7-8" in diameter; lined with vegetation

Eggs: average clutch 6-15; pale green to white; 1 brood per year

Young: hatch in 26-30 days; eyes open; completely mobile and able to swim; capable of flight at 60 days

Predators: fox, skunk, raccoon and coyote prey on eggs; turtles, large fish and domestic cat prey on nestlings

Migration: present year-round; birds disperse across Arizona each fall

Description: The male Mallard is gray with a distinct green head, thin white collar, rust-colored chest, yellow bill and orange legs. The female is a drab, mottled brown with a orange bill.

birds

DID YOU KNOW...? Birds, especially males, communic: vocally more than any other species of wildlife. Birds typic: use songs to attract mates or defend territory. Calls : uncomplicated sounds that are used to communicate dan; or feeding. Both Eastern and Western Meadowlarks live Arizona, and though they look almost identical, they can distinguished from each other by song.

MEADOWLARK, WESTERN
Sturnella neglecta

Size: body 8-11" long; 14¾" wingspan; 3 oz.

abitat: meadows, grasslands and agricultural areas

Range: throughout Arizona

Food: insects and seeds

Mating: early spring

Nest: ground nest; cup-shaped and constructed of grasses

Eggs: average clutch 3-7; white spotted with brown and purple; 2 broods common

Young: hatch blind and featherless in 13-15 days; eyes open at approximately 1 week; leave the nest at 12 days

ators: snake, ground squirrel, badger, coyote and raptors (birds of prey)

ration: present year-round in the north; some birds disperse into southern Arizona in winter

cription: The Western Meadowlark is buff to brown streaky black markings, bright yellow undersides and a inent black V on its chest. It has a slender face and bill. nale and female are similar in appearance.

birds

DID YOU KNOW...? A single Great Horned Owl can ca
nearly 1,000 mice each year. Its diet is the most diverse o
North American owls. It has the strongest talons of all
species. The Great Horned Owl is nicknamed the tiger v
wings, because it can kill mammals as large as skunks a
porcupines.

OWL, GREAT HORNED
Bubo virginianus

Size: body 18-25" long; 4-5' wingspan; 3 lbs.

Habitat: open wooded areas, woodlots near agricultural areas and deserts

Range: throughout Arizona

Food: small mammals such as mice and skunks, smaller owls, waterfowl and other birds, reptiles and insects; regurgitates pellets of indigestible parts of prey

Mating: December to May

Nest: abandoned nests of hawks, squirrels and crows and in tree hollows

Eggs: average clutch 1-5; white; male brings food to female while she tends the eggs; 1 brood per year

Young: hatch blind and covered with fine down in 28-32 days; eyes open at 7-10 days; young gain flight feathers at 6-9 weeks

Predators: Golden Eagle and Northern Goshawk; harassed by crows and jays

Duration: present year-round

Description: The Great Horned Owl is a large, reddish brown to gray or black owl with lighter, streaked undersides. It has a white throat collar, yellow eyes and horn-like tufts of feathers on its head. It relies on its keen senses of hearing and sight to find its prey.

birds

DID YOU KNOW...? Like all predatory birds, the sn Burrowing Owl has strong, razor sharp talons for catching prey. Typically, the Burrowing Owl swallows its prey whole, it must later regurgitate pellets (the indigestible portio including fur, bones, etc.) Female and young Burrowing O can deter predators from entering their burrow by makin sound similar to that of a rattlesnake. Unlike most other ov the Burrowing Owl is active during the day.

OWL, WESTERN BURROWING
Athene cunicularia hypugaea

Size: body 8-9¾" long; 21-22" wingspan; 5-8 oz.

Habitat: grasslands and dry prairies around prairie dog towns

Range: throughout Arizona

Food: insects, small mammals, reptiles, other birds and carrion (remains of dead animals)

Mating: March to August with peak activity during April and May

Nest: occupies an abandoned burrow; will utilize artificial nesting structures

Eggs: average clutch 3-11; white; 1 brood per year

Young: hatch in 21-28 days covered with soft, grayish down; female feeds the young regurgitated meat; young leave the nest at 28 days; independent at 8-10 weeks

Predators: hawk and eagle; fox, raccoon, coyote, snake, domestic dog and cat prey on eggs and nestlings

Migration: most migrate in winter, though many remain in southern Arizona

Description: The Burrowing Owl is often seen on fence or burrow mounds. It is brown with white spots, lighter undersides with brown barring and a prominent white chinstrap. It has long legs, large yellow eyes and a flat-topped head. The male is slightly larger than the female.

underground burrow

birds

female

DID YOU KNOW...? A popular game bird, the Gambel's Qu
is named for renowned naturalist William Gambel (18
1849). During the winter, they gather in groups called cove
which are usually made up of 20 birds each. At night, t
Gambel's Quail roosts in shrubs 3' off the ground. Like m
quail species, the Gambel's Quail avoids danger by runni
for cover or by short bursts of flight usually less than 100'. T
quail is pictured on the logo for the Arizona Game and F
Department.

QUAIL, GAMBEL'S
Callipepla gambelii

Size: body 8-11" long; 14" wingspan; 6 oz.

Habitat: desert thickets, pinyon-juniper forests and shrub land; usually near water

Range: northwest, central and southern Arizona

Food: seeds, grasses, cacti fruit, grains and insects

Mating: March

Nest: shallow bowl-shaped ground nest; lined with grasses; usually near cover

Eggs: average clutch 12-14; buff to off-white; 1-2 broods each year

Young: hatch in 23 days with feathers and able to feed themselves; leave the nest at 10 days

Predators: bobcat, owl, hawk, coyote, fox and reptiles; Greater Roadrunners prey on eggs and young

Migration: present year-round

Description: The Gambel's Quail is chunky, pear-shaped and mostly gray with light buff undersides. It has short, rounded wings and short legs. The male has a black throat and face, red cap, white head band and distinctive topknot plumage.

birds

DID YOU KNOW...? The American Robin uses anting to itself of lice and other parasites. The bird positions itself n an anthill and allows ants to crawl all over its body. Robins not listening for worms when they cock their heads from s to side. Because their eyes are placed far back on the side their heads, they must turn their heads from side to side look at things.

ROBIN, AMERICAN
Turdus migratorius

Size: body 9-11" long; 17" wingspan; 2-3 oz.

Habitat: Arizona's mountains, wooded areas and riparian areas

Range: central, northern and southeastern Arizona

Food: earthworms, insects, fruits and berries

Mating: spring

Nest: females build nests out of mud, grass and twigs; found in trees, shrubs and artificial structures

Eggs: average clutch 3-5; pale blue; 2 broods per year

Young: hatch blind and featherless in 12-14 days; eyes open at 1 week; flight feathers develop at 13-20 days

Predators: Merlin (winter only), Sharp-shinned Hawk, Cooper's Hawk, Northern Goshawk and domestic cat

Migration: present year-round; birds move around Arizona in winter

Description: Male American Robins have slate-gray backs, rusty red chests and white speckled throats. Females are gray-brown with pale orange chests. They form large migrating flocks in the fall.

birds

DID YOU KNOW...? Abert's Towhee is a relatively shy bi[rd] although, like many birds, it is extremely territorial during [the] mating season and defends its area against intruders. Territ[ory] is generally a small area located within the animal's hor[ne] range where it locates food, water and cover. Territorial displa[ys] by birds are vocal in nature and conducted largely by male[s]

101

TOWHEE, ABERT'S
Pipilo aberti

Size: body 8-9½" long; 11" wingspan; 1.6 oz.

Habitat: dense brush (mesquite, cottonwood and ironwood) near foothills and streams; residential areas

Range: south central Arizona; isolated populations in northwest Arizona

Food: insects and seeds; ground feeder

Mating: April to June

Nest: open, cup-shaped nest constructed 4-12' above ground in bushes or trees

Eggs: average clutch 2-4; light blue-green; 2 broods per year

Young: hatch blind and featherless in 10-12 days; eyes open at approximately 1 week; flight feathers develop at 10 days; leave the nest at 12-13 days

Predators: Cooper's Hawk, domestic cat; fox, raccoon and snake prey on eggs and nestlings

Migration: present year-round

Description: Abert's Towhee is a stocky, sparrow-like bird. Grayish brown to chestnut brown with lighter undersides. Has a black facemask, a light colored cone-shaped bill and a long tail. The male and female are similar in appearance.

birds

DID YOU KNOW...? Wild Turkeys commonly form flocks o[f] or more birds and roost in trees each evening. In sprir[g] males perform elaborate courtship displays to attract femal[e] In 1782, it lost by a single vote to the Bald Eagle as t[he] national bird. In 1900 the Wild Turkey population was ab[out] 30,000 due to habitat loss. Today, thanks to better wild[life] management, Wild Turkey numbers have grown to nearly [a] million nationwide.

TURKEY, WILD
Meleagris gallopavo

Size: body 3-4' long; 5' wingspan; males 18-20 lbs.; females 9-11 lbs.

Habitat: ponderosa pine and mixed conifer forests

Range: north and east central Arizona; small populations in southern Arizona

Food: seeds, grass, insects, fruits, acorns, pinyon nuts, pine seeds and juniper berries

Mating: March to May

Nest: hens build nest on the ground, usually a leaf-lined hollow in heavy brush

Eggs: average clutch 7-13; buff with tan markings; 1 brood per year

Young: hatch in 28 days covered with feathers and able to feed themselves; able to fly at 2-4 weeks; remain with female for up to 4 months

Predators: mountain lion, bear, coyote, bobcat, domestic dog, gray fox, hawk and owl; raccoon and skunk prey on eggs and young

Migration: present year-round

Description: The Wild Turkey is a large, dark brown and black bird with fan tail. Males have wattles (fleshy growths that hang beneath the chin), spurs (bony projections on the back of each leg), a snood (a flap of skin that drapes over the bill), and a hair-like chest beard. Females are more drab. They are strong short-distance flyers.

birds

soaring

DID YOU KNOW...? The Turkey Vulture is commonly call[ed] turkey buzzard. It soars effortlessly for hours on wings held [in] a slight V-shape. It roosts in groups and is commonly se[en] feeding on roadside carcasses. Unlike most birds, the Turk[ey] Vulture appears to have a keen sense of smell, which it us[es] as it scavenges for carrion. It is still unknown how vultures c[an] feed on the remains of an animal that died of infectious d[is-]ease without becoming ill themselves.

VULTURE, TURKEY
Cathartes aura

Size: body 26-32" long; 6' wingspan; 4 lbs.

Habitat: deserts, open woodlands, pastures, brush land and roadsides

Range: throughout Arizona

Food: carrion (remains of dead animals); occasionally prey on live, helpless animals

Mating: early spring

Nest: no real nest constructed; eggs laid on the ground and cliffsides and in rock crevices, caves and hollowed tree stumps

Eggs: average clutch 2; white with brown blotches; 1 brood per year

Young: hatch in 38-41 days; adults feed the young regurgitated food; able to fly at 10 weeks

Predators: raccoons prey on eggs

Migration: most migrate in winter, though some remain in extreme southern Arizona

Description: The Turkey Vulture is blackish brown with long, two-tone wings and a long, squared tail. It has a distinctive featherless red head and a hooked ivory bill. It has short, sturdy legs and yellow feet well adapted to walking and running.

no nest

birds

female

DID YOU KNOW...? The Gila Woodpecker is comm
throughout much of Arizona. Like all woodpeckers, it has
chisel-like bill used for drilling into trees in search of insec
It has strong legs and toes to cling to trees and a stiffened t
which serves to prop it up while it climbs and drills. It also h
specialized skull bones to absorb the shock of drilling and
spear-like tongue adapted for catching insects.

WOODPECKER, GILA
Melanerpes uropygialis

Size: body 8-10" long; 16" wingspan; 2.3 oz.

Habitat: desert and scrub land; usually containing saguaro cactus or cottonwood, willow or mesquite trees

Range: central and southern Arizona

Food: insects, bird eggs, fruits and berries

Mating: early spring and summer

Nest: cavity nest; usually located 15-25' above ground; often in saguaro cactus or cottonwood, willow or mesquite trees

Eggs: average clutch 3-5; white; 2 broods common

Young: hatch blind and featherless at 12-14 days; eyes open at approximately 1 week; feathers develop within 20 days

Predators: Cooper's Hawk, Sharp-shinned Hawk; European Starling may destroy eggs and take over nest

Migration: present year-round

Description: The Gila Woodpecker is tan to gray with dark wing. The male has a red cap. The female is similar in appearance but has no red cap.

birds

DID YOU KNOW...? The Cactus Wren is a very inquisiti[ve] bird, commonly investigating intruders in its territory includi[ng] cars and campers. The male and female may build multi[ple] nests for roosting, raising young and as a decoy against pred[a]tors. Unlike most wren species, it does not hold its tail in [a] cocked and upright position. *Campylorhynchus* is Greek [for] curved beak. The Cactus Wren was named the State Bird [of] Arizona in 1931. It is the largest wren species in the U.S.

WREN, CACTUS
Campylorhynchus brunneicapillus

Size: body 6½-9" long; 11" wingspan; 1.4 oz.

Habitat: arid regions, foothills, desert and scrub land containing yucca, mesquite, ironweed and cholla cactus

Range: extreme northwest, central and southern Arizona

Food: insects (ants, beetles, grasshoppers and wasps), fruit, seeds and reptiles; relies on the juice of insects for moisture

Mating: March to September

Nest: bulky, football-shaped nest constructed of grasses and lined with feathers; most commonly located in cholla cactus or thorny shrubs including mesquite and ironwood

Eggs: average clutch 4-5; white with reddish spots; 2 or more broods per year

Young: hatch in 16 days; leave the nest at 19-23 days; independent at 50 days

Predators: shrike and domestic cat; snakes prey on eggs and young

Migration: present year-round

Description: The Cactus Wren is mostly grayish brown black and white spots and streaks, brown cap, black t area, dark legs and lighter, spotted undersides.

birds

LIFELIST

Place a check by each mammal or bird you've s
whether in your backyard, on a camping trip or at the

Critters

☐ **Badger**

Location: _____ Date: ___

Comments: _____

☐ **Bat, Occult Little Brown**

Location: _____ Date: ___

Comments: _____

☐ **Bear, Black**

Location: _____ Date: ___

Comments: _____

☐ **Beaver**

Location: _____ Date: ___

Comments: _____

☐ **Bobcat**

Location: _____ Date: ___

Comments: _____

☐ **Cottontail, Desert**

Location: _____ Date: ___

Comments: _____

☐ **Coyote**

Location: _____ Date: ___

Comments: _____

☐ **Deer, Mule**

Location: _____ Date: ___

Comments: _____

Deer, White-tailed
Location: _____ Date: _____
Comments: _____

Elk
Location: _____ Date: _____
Comments: _____

Fox, Gray
Location: _____ Date: _____
Comments: _____

Jackrabbit, Black-tailed
Location: _____ Date: _____
Comments: _____

Javelina
Location: _____ Date: _____
Comments: _____

Lion, Mountain
Location: _____ Date: _____
Comments: _____

Muskrat
Location: _____ Date: _____
Comments: _____

Otter, River
Location: _____ Date: _____
Comments: _____

Porcupine
Location: _____ Date: _____
Comments: _____

☐ **Pronghorn**

Location: _____ Date: ___

Comments: _____

☐ **Raccoon**

Location: _____ Date: ___

Comments: _____

☐ **Ringtail**

Location: _____ Date: ___

Comments: _____

☐ **Sheep, Desert Bighorn**

Location: _____ Date: ___

Comments: _____

☐ **Skunk, Striped**

Location: _____ Date: ___

Comments: _____

☐ **Squirrel, Round-tailed Ground**

Location: _____ Date: ___

Comments: _____

☐ **Wolf, Mexican Gray**

Location: _____ Date: ___

Comments: _____

☐ **Woodrat, White-throated**

Location: _____ Date: ___

Comments: _____

❻

Blackbird, Red-winged
Location: _____ Date: _____
Comments: _____

Bluebird, Mountain
Location: _____ Date: _____
Comments: _____

Condor, California
Location: _____ Date: _____
Comments: _____

Coot, American
Location: _____ Date: _____
Comments: _____

Crane, Sandhill
Location: _____ Date: _____
Comments: _____

Dove, Mourning
Location: _____ Date: _____
Comments: _____

Eagle, Bald
Location: _____ Date: _____
Comments: _____

Falcon, Peregrine
Location: _____ Date: _____
Comments: _____

Hawk, Cooper's
Location: _____ Date: _____
Comments: _____

☐ **Hawk, Red-tailed**
  Location: _____ Date: __
  Comments: _____

☐ **Hawk, Sharp-shinned**
  Location: _____ Date: __
  Comments: _____

☐ **Heron, Great Blue**
  Location: _____ Date: __
  Comments: _____

☐ **Hummingbird, Anna's**
  Location: _____ Date: __
  Comments: _____

☐ **Kestrel, American**
  Location: _____ Date: __
  Comments: _____

☐ **Mallard**
  Location: _____ Date: __
  Comments: _____

☐ **Meadowlark, Western**
  Location: _____ Date: __
  Comments: _____

☐ **Owl, Great Horned**
  Location: _____ Date: __
  Comments: _____

Owl, Western Burrowing
Location: _____ Date: _____
Comments: _____

Quail, Gambel's
Location: _____ Date: _____
Comments: _____

Robin, American
Location: _____ Date: _____
Comments: _____

Towhee, Abert's
Location: _____ Date: _____
Comments: _____

Turkey, Wild
Location: _____ Date: _____
Comments: _____

Vulture, Turkey
Location: _____ Date: _____
Comments: _____

Woodpecker, Gila
Location: _____ Date: _____
Comments: _____

Wren, Cactus
Location: _____ Date: _____
Comments: _____

WILD WORDS

A

Adaptation: a particular characteristic developed by a plant or mal that makes it better suited to its environment.

Amphibians: cold-blooded, smooth-skinned vertebrates that s part of their life on land and part of their life in the water in ing frogs, toads, newts and salamanders.

Anthropomorphism: attributing human characteristics to anim

Antler: bony projections grown and shed each year by membe the deer family, typically males. Antlers are used in cour rivalries between competing males.

B

Behavior: the way in which an animal responds to its environr

Brood: (noun) the offspring of birds hatched at one time; (ve hatch, protect and warm the young, usually done instinctive the female.

Browse: (noun) portions of woody plants including twigs, s and leaves used as food by animals such as deer; (verb) parts of woody plants.

Buck: a male deer, goat, pronghorn or rabbit.

Bull: a male moose, elk or bison.

Burrow: (noun) a hole, tunnel or underground den excavated animal for shelter or refuge; (verb) to dig underground.

C

Camouflage: a protective adaptation that enables an animal t guise itself or blend with its surroundings.

Carnivore: an animal that eats other animals; a meat eater.

on: the body of a dead animal in the natural state of decay, ich serves as a food source for other animals.

h: a nest of eggs.

blooded (ectothermic): an animal whose body temperature is pendent upon and varies with the temperature of its environ-nt (e.g., fish, amphibians and reptiles).

nunication: sound, scent or behavior recognized by members he same species.

etition: different species of animals that use the same source food or shelter.

ervation: the care, wise use and management of a resource.

mer: an animal that gets its food from producers (plants).

ship: a behavior or series of actions an animal displays to indi-e to the opposite sex that it is ready to mate in order to roduce.

: naturally-occurring sheltered areas that provide conceal-nt and shelter for wildlife, such as a dead tree, fallen log, rock crops, dense areas of brush or trees.

a female moose, wapiti (elk) or bison.

scular: active in twilight at dawn and dusk.

al: active during the day.

a female deer, pronghorn or rabbit.

a layer of soft, fine feathers that provides insulation.

a male duck.

E

Ecology: the study of the relationships between living things the environments in which they live.

Ecosystem: an interacting system of plants, animals, soil an mactic conditions in a self-contained environment (e.g., p marsh, swamp, lake or stream).

Endangered: a species in danger of becoming extinct due to d(ing population numbers.

Environment: the entire surroundings of an organism (plant o mal) or group of organisms.

Estuary: area where fresh water and salt water meet.

Ethics: principles of good conduct; a sense of right and wror

Exotic: a foreign species introduced to an area from another r(or ecosystem. Exotic species are considered undesirable a; compete with native species for habitat and food.

Extinct: a species that no longer exists or has died out.

F

Fledgling: young birds learning to fly.

Food chain: plants and animals linked together as sources consumers of food; typically an organism higher in the chain eats one lower in the food chain, so the health of (dependent on the health of another.

Food web: the many possible feeding relationships found wi\ given ecosystem.

Forage: (noun) plant material such as grasses, ferns, shrub; the leaves and twigs of trees; (verb) to eat plant material.

species: wildlife that can be hunted or trapped according to
al seasons and limits.

tion: length of pregnancy.

at enhancement: the development and improvement of habi-
(including sources of food, water, cover and space) for the
nefit of fish or wildlife.

tat: the local environment in which an animal lives.
mponents include food, water, cover (shelter) and space.

a female pheasant, duck, quail or turkey.

vore: an animal that eats only plant material.

nation: a period of winter dormancy during which an animal
ws its body processes dramatically, reducing the amount of
ergy required for survival. True hibernators can slow their
dy processes nearly to a stop, requiring much less energy to
vive. Partial hibernators do not reduce their body processes
much, are more easily awakened and meet their relatively
her energy requirements by means such as storing fat.

range: the area over which an animal repeatedly travels in
ler to locate food, water and cover.

hard protrusions that continuously grow on the head of cer-
mammals such as the bighorn sheep and bison. Horns are
de of keratin, the same material that makes fingernails.

ate: to warm eggs (usually bird eggs) with body heat so they
velop and hatch. Females typically incubate the eggs.

Introduced species: a plant or animal brought from another re often another continent, either intentionally or by accident; duced species can have positive or negative effects on the r species. Also referred to as "exotic" or "non-native," espe when the result is negative.

Invertebrates: animals without backbones, including ins earthworms and jellyfish.

J-L

Land ethic: deliberate, thoughtful and responsible consideratic the natural landscape and natural resources, including wi fossil fuels, soil, water and timber.

Land management: the purposeful manipulation of land or ha by people to encourage wildlife populations to incr decrease or stabilize in number. In the case of wildlife involves managing food, water, cover and space to affect p lation numbers.

M

Mammal: a warm-blooded animal that has fur or hair and prod milk to feed its young.

Migration: the seasonal movements of fish and wildlife from area to another usually triggered by length of daylight h Animals that move varying distances at irregular times de dent upon weather and availability of food are partial migra Animals that move to the same places at the same times year are complete migrators.

N

Native: an indigenous or naturally-occurring species of pla animal.

Natural resource: materials found in nature to which people assigned value such as timber, fresh water, wildlife and fuels (coal and oil).

:urnal: an animal that is active by night.

game species: the majority of wildlife not hunted by humans cluding songbirds, raptors, reptiles and amphibians.

enewable resources: nonliving natural resources which, for all actical purposes, cannot be replaced, including metallic min-als, such as gold and copper, and fossil fuels, such as coal d oil.

ivore: an animal that eats both plants and animals (meat).

rtunist: an animal that can take advantage of any number of od sources available.

omone: a chemical scent secreted as a means of communi-tion between members of the same species.

osynthesis: the process by which plant cells convert light, ter and carbon dioxide into energy and nutrients while simul-eously releasing oxygen.

age: the feathers of a bird.

tion: toxic (poisonous) substances deposited in the air, water soil creating an unhealthy environment.

lation: a collection of individuals of the same species in a en area whose members can breed with one another.

ator: an animal that hunts and feeds on other animals (prey).

an animal hunted or killed for food by other animals (predators).

ucers: plants that obtain energy from the sun and produce d through the process of photosynthesis.

e: the particular geographic region in which a species is found.

Raptor: a bird of prey including falcons, owls, eagles, hawks ospreys.

Recreation: an activity undertaken for enjoyment; entertainr often associated with natural resources (water, forests, rock mations) includes rock climbing, bird watching, fish canoeing and hunting.

Renewable natural resource: a natural resource that can be rep ished and harvested, including trees and wildlife.

Reptile: cold-blooded vertebrate animals that lay eggs (snakes, lizards and turtles).

Riparian area: lands adjacent to streams, rivers, lakes and c wetlands where the vegetation is influenced by the great a ability of water.

Roost: refers to a safe gathering place used by wildlife, us birds and bats, for rest or sleep.

Rut: activity associated with breeding behavior.

S

Scat: refers to defecation, excrement or waste.

Scavenger: an animal that feeds on the remains of dead anin

Scrape: an area where concentrated amounts of urine are n with mud to attract a mate or indicate territory.

Season: time of year when game species may be legally harve

Sow: a female bear.

Species: a group of animals that have similar structure, com ancestors and characteristics they maintain through breed

Stewardship: responsible care of natural resources for future erations.

ng: the artificial propagation and introduction of game cies into an area.

ry: the area an animal will defend, usually during breeding son, against intruders of its own species.

tened: a classification for wildlife species whose population is reat decline and approaching the "endangered" classifica-

rates: animals with a backbone, including fish, birds, mam-s, reptiles and amphibians.

-blooded (endothermic): an animal whose body temperature nrelated to its environment (e.g., mammals and birds).

(noun) young that no longer depend on an adult for food; b) to withhold mother's milk from young and substitute other rishment.

fe: non-domesticated plants and animals (including mam-s, birds, fish, reptiles, insects and amphibians).

e agency: a state or federal organization responsible for aging wildlife.

e management: a combination of techniques, scientific wledge and technical skills used to protect, conserve and age wildlife and habitat.

kill: the death of animals during winter resulting from lack od and exposure to cold.

WILDLIFE FOREVER PROJEC
IN ARIZONA

Working at the grassroots level, Wildlife Forever (WF
completed conservation projects in all 50 states.

- Worked with the Arizona Game and Fish Departm
  develop a recovery program for threatened So
  pronghorn along the Arizona-Mexico border. W
  Forever helped with the research necessary in formu
  the plan, including aerial surveys.

- Constructed 3,000 bass shelters, 2,520 catfish h
  and 150 tire towers for placement in Lake Havasu.
  artificial shelters helped to offset the lack of natural
  for the bass, crappie and catfish in the lake, incre
  populations of these and other popular sport fish sp

- Improved habitat for largemouth bass, smallmouth
  and crappie on Bartlett Lake in Tonto National F
  Sixty-nine artificial fish houses were constructed, cr
  a total of 23 different complexes that were placed thr
  out the lake.

- Restored wintering and migratory habitat for ma
  blue-winged teal, pintails and shorebirds within In
  National Wildlife Refuge by clearing and controlling
  vegetation and rehabilitating five shallow marshes
  refuge.

- Added fish habitat structures to more than 40 co
  Lake Havasu, encompassing over 875 surface ac
  order to improve fish habitat for crappies, bass an
  fish. In addition, the newly-created habitat has
  credited with helping save two endangered species o
  the Bonytail Chub and the Razorback Sucker.

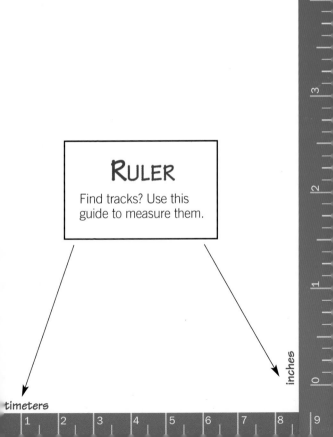

RULER

Find tracks? Use this guide to measure them.

inches

timeters